Make F.I.T. Your Purpose

ISARD HAASAKKER

For my wife.

DISCLAIMER

The core objective of this book is to translate my experience into valuable advice to save you time and money when implementing SAP ERP. That is why this book is based on true events. All names in my stories have been changed, so similarities to real individuals is pure coincidental. In some instances, a collection of occurrences which were years apart and took place in different locations have been written as if they happen during one project, to facilitate your understanding of the story and the wider point it highlights.

Still, I want to point out that some events did really happen.

Was I involved in a project to implement SAP ERP within three months?
Yes.

Was my task during that project to configure all logistical business flows?
Absolutely.

Was that experience the basis to learn how to configure a working SAP ERP system, including accounting and logistics, within one working day?
Certainly.

ACKNOWLEDGMENTS

I would like to express my gratitude to the many people who saw me through this book; to all those who provided support, talked things over, read, wrote, offered comments, allowed me to quote their remarks and assisted in the editing, proofreading and design.

Special thanks to Dan Sullivan, Jason Clarke and Peter Thompson.

My dad taught me a wise lesson. He always focused on seeking job satisfaction, as that is the true foundation for a successful career.
Thanks for this wonderful insight.

This book was written in collaboration with Write Business Results, who specialise in business book writing and book marketing.
To discuss your business book requirements, contact owner and director Georgia Kirke at info@writebusinessresults.com, or visit www.writebusinessresults.com.

CONTENTS

INTRODUCTION

Many years ago, I walked into an empty office that was lit by the British morning sun. While my laptop was starting up, I greeted other early birds in the kitchenette. Time to pour my first cup of tea of the day. We chatted about the latest football scores and exchanged some celebrity gossip. But how was I to know that my life was about to change forever? To me it was business as usual.

Later that morning, Mike came to my desk. Immediately I noticed that he was wearing a tie that is usually hidden away in his drawer. This must be a special occasion, I thought. He asked whether I would like to join him for a meeting. That sounded rather intriguing. We took the elevator to the top floor. That is where the senior management were hiding. Finally I got my opportunity to see it with my own eyes. Colleagues said that it had only a few spacious, luxurious rooms with plenty of daylight pouring in. And they were right. This does not compare to our open office, housing countless hot desks. Walking towards the executive lounge that morning made me feel very special.

The meeting room could easily accommodate 20 people but this time it was only occupied by one immaculately dressed man. It made me feel like the odd one out. However, he was very friendly towards me and certainly did not waste a second in revealing his objectives.

"Mr Haasakker, thank you. Come in and have a seat".

He introduced himself as Peter and explained about an exciting new project. One that presented potential to make a huge impact on their business. It has to be completed on time, as the licence for their current systems would soon expire. He had wanted SAP for a long time and explained that now was the time to take the big leap forward. He went on to proffer that this was a high profile implementation and only the best team resources would be offered an opportunity to take part.

It was obvious that Peter meant business. He was visiting our office to finalise the contract and to meet the team. However, one seat was still available. Both Mike and Peter were very eager for me to come on board. Peter quickly added that all the preparation could be done at my current desk and only a few weeks on site was required to provide training and support.

Mike chimed in with a few minor details and wrapped up with, "So, Isard, this is a great next step for you. Based on the work you've done for us so far, we think you would be perfect for the job. We're making the necessary arrangements for you as we speak [dramatic pause]...if you're up to it, that is?"

I looked at Peter and smiled. That seemed to seal the deal. Before words had even formed in my head, Mike slapped me on the back and added, "Great, I knew you wouldn't let us down. Welcome to the team. You have three months to get all logistics flows ready for go-live. In the meantime, you'd better make sure your passport is valid for a trip to Dubai."

Huh?

Either they had failed to mention this from the outset, or the whole meeting had gone so fast I didn't hear. I realised that I had just agreed to configure planning, procurement, sales and transportation for a company in Dubai. Three months before the system is going to be used to run their business and no wiggle room as their current systems were being shelved regardless. On top of that, data needed to be migrated and end user training material had to be produced. There was no time to lose. Sheer panic took hold of me, and Mike must have noticed. He quickly grabbed my shoulder and guided me out of the room, whilst smiling to Peter.

Luckily it was about lunch time. A good moment for a walk outside. After pacing back and forth in the car park for several minutes, I decided to take on the challenge with enthusiasm. Sure, I had a degree of concern about the timescales. It seemed like mission impossible. Nonetheless I knuckled down for the next twelve weeks to get ready, then flew out to Dubai for the cut-over weekend (the weekend before go-live, aiming to get the system ready for the users at 6am on a Monday morning) and go-live celebrations. It was both exciting and manic but everyone put their heads down and focussed with laser-like precision on the fixed deadline.

Before I knew it, my plane left Dubai to fly back home. For the first time I was able to relax. We've done it, I marvelled. We had achieved what I and many others had deemed impossible. We delivered on a project rife with complexities within a tight timeframe. The business was ecstatic. The client was happy. I was absolutely shattered. But nothing beats that sense of accomplishment you get when you've put blood, sweat and tears into something that turns out to be a success.

Later in my career, I realised that the Dubai challenge was very special indeed. As a team we had managed to do something that was unheard of at the time. It is also still considered impossible by many CIO's and senior program managers. Five months! The more I reflected on my experience in Dubai, the more I began to wonder what, specifically, made it work. I identified the essential moving parts and the unnecessary ones too, and created a process that could actually streamline that project even further. The results of my assessment are the basis of my career and for this book.

This book is divided into three parts.

Part One explains the Enterprise Resource Planning (ERP) concept. Then SAP is contextualised as an ERP software solution and the current undisputed worldwide market leader. You do not need prior knowledge of ERP or SAP to get an understanding of the functionality available.

Part Two will introduce the **Fast Implementation Track™ (FIT)**. Every chapter will explain and break down each of the FIT components. These are crucial and will enable you to implement SAP ERP on time and within budget.

Finally, Part Three summarises the key points by using a real life story.

This book is written for all project stakeholders.

First of all, this book reaches out to all entrepreneurs with the desire to implement an ERP system for their business. Your aim is to implement such an IT system on time and within budget. You might not have the technical knowledge, but you have a clear vision of what you want to achieve with ERP. Most likely you currently project your expectations based on the daily activities of your personnel, as well as the interaction with your suppliers and clients. From this book, you can expect to avoid any technical jargon (or at least it will be explained) and I will give you the tools and insights you need to avoid money being wasted unnecessarily.

Secondly, any top and middle management with budget responsibility get the opportunity to explore the mind of the entrepreneurs who provide the money to implement an ERP system. Understanding the business leaders will equip you to make the best possible decisions on project delivery, and new ways of thinking about the project which can lead to enhanced communication with the steering committee. Feeling like you have to beg for additional funding is the last thing you want to experience. Instead you want to be seen as the person that successfully executes the vision of the entrepreneur.

Lastly, those employees and contractors doing the

actual work are not forgotten. You are the ones on the ground, making it happen. You have the power to make the ERP implementation a success. Knowing the vision of the entrepreneur is a crucial step towards securing that end result. Awareness of budget pressures is vital. But in the end, you are at the heart of the project's success.

Introducing an ERP system requires very knowledgeable professionals. In order to work successfully on an ERP project, you have to be able to excel beyond your core duties within the project. Sometimes employees can see this as doing extra work for no extra money. But it is important for your employability and future income that you build a reputation that you have the capability to analyse, design and test full end-to-end business scenarios. Only then you match the expectation of the entrepreneur and add value.

During my career as an SAP consultant, I was only one single voice within a large team. My suggestions for prevention, improvement and damage mitigation were often neglected. Most times I was kindly reminded that I was not part of management. My task was to consult and not to decide. So I made up my mind to write this book to allow me a voice. My drive to save you time and money hopefully gets your attention. In reading this book, you are giving me the opportunity to demystify the horror stories. The common sense laid out in this book gives you the confidence that your SAP ERP implementation projects can indeed run smoothly, on time and within budget.

Make F.I.T. Your Purpose is written for entrepreneurs, CEOs, CIOs, program managers and consultants alike, particularly those who are involved with expensive SAP ERP implementation projects. If you have budget responsibility, this book will arm you with the knowledge and power to save your company millions of pounds and increase its overall efficiency and productivity. If you are a small or medium-sized business owner, you will understand how you can implement SAP ERP using a modest budget.

If you are a program manager or consultant, this book is an essential learning opportunity to step into the mind of the members of the steering committee. They are funding the project and are ultimately responsible for success.

The aim of this book is to create a universal language and frame of reference for any SAP ERP implementation. Please enjoy the information contained within, and reach out with your questions after reading!

PART ONE

1 ENTERPRISE RESOURCE PLANNING (E.R.P.)

After my fateful morning with Mike and Peter, the enormity of the challenge became ever so clear. There were only two people in the team. Justin was appointed to handle all the accounting and it was up to me to do the logistics. Immediately after lunch I walked over to Justin. He told me that he had just returned from seeing Peter. Apparently he'd had the same experience as me. Overwhelmed by the situation and agreeing to help out before knowing all the details. You could see that he was still bewildered. At least I'd had a bit more time to come to terms with it.

Mike then asked us both to see Peter again, as he wanted to provide some insights into the core business processes. It ended up taking the entire afternoon. There was so much information to take in over a relatively short period of time. It was almost impossible to write it all down. There was a lot for me to cover. Of course, you had the standard procurement and sales processes. But some were relatively new to me, such as consignment and subcontracting. Quite complex pricing arrangements were made and some clients had rebate agreements. And every night the system needed to evaluate stock levels to trigger replenishment.

Justin had his hands full with constructing a chart of accounts, ensuring bank transfers and direct debits were processed automatically every night. Value Added Tax needed to be paid periodically. The management wanted to perform a profitability analysis on their sales and purchases. And that was just at the top of his to-do list.

Peter wanted a system allowing you to plan when stock needs to be procured or manufactured. You could register customer sales orders and all their subsequent documents required to complete the associated business processes. You could review current stock levels, and whether they were freely available to clients, blocked for trade or requiring quality inspection. Every step in the process allowed you to issue document output to inform your suppliers and clients. Reports had to be available that allowed your departments to make operational decisions based on open orders and deliveries. It also had to be possible to verify whether your goods movements had an associated invoice, and whether this invoice had been paid. When necessary, dunning letters were to be issued to remind you that certain payments were overdue.

Later that evening I found myself at the bar in my hotel, tired but excited. Fearful but surprisingly upbeat. Never in my life did I have such mixed feelings. It took me quite a while to get to sleep.

The following weeks passed so quickly. Almost immediately we realised that we could not work in isolation. Even though the logistics business transactions seemed to take centre stage, many financial postings were needed back stage. Logistics and accounting go hand in hand. For example, any change of stock ownership triggers a financial posting at the same time. Any minuscule misalignment between logistics and accounting prevents the entire business transaction from being registered. Especially in the beginning, any step in the process grounded to a halt because accounting and logistics were not properly connected. It was a race against time, but we got it all working like a well oiled machine a few days before we 'went live'.

We were ready to meet the main objective to replace various stand alone IT systems into one integrated accounting and logistics system. Immediately improving both operational efficiency and productivity dramatically. This is essentially the main goal for any Enterprise Resource Planning system.

Enterprise Resource Planning (ERP) allows you to run your business within one single database. You always have accurate information immediately available as all departments share the same data. So when you place an order with your supplier, your order desk can inform the customer when new stock is likely to be available without contacting other departments.

Nowadays, ERP functionality is considered the norm by your suppliers and clients. When you place an order online you expect accurate stock information, a reliable assessment of the delivery date and updates of the progress of delivery. So when you have found the goods you wish to buy, added them to your basket, entered your details at the checkout and placed your order, you would surely be surprised to then receive an apologetic email the next day stating that your ordered goods are not in stock.

When you experience this, it is a sign that you are dealing with a company with many independent IT systems in place to run the core business processes. There is no integration between sales, procurement, stock control and accounting. Data between systems needs to be transferred several times a day instead, so the information you see on the website at any one time may or may not be an accurate reflection of reality.

ERP projects have large-scale implications for both the back stage and the front stage of a business. There is a consensus between the steering committee, program managers and consultants that these are time consuming and complicated projects. Consequently, they all expect that it costs an arm and a leg to implement.

I'm here to challenge those assumptions.

My Dubai project experience allows me to share with you what I know to be true: you can implement ERP significantly faster than people deemed feasible. Just for reference, the scope of the Dubai project took me initially two months to configure. Now I can achieve the same within one working day! The reason for this immense reduction of time is directly linked to refining the **Fast Implementation Track™ (F.I.T.)**, explained in more detail later in this book.

So when staying on the **Fast Implementation Track™**, you can save millions of pounds. And the best example to prove this statement, is to apply it to SAP.

2 SYSTEM ANALYSIS AND PROGRAM DEVELOPMENT (S.A.P.)

Years after my Dubai adventure, I went back for a short holiday. Some of my colleagues were still there and we met to reminisce. The next day I was enjoying the warm sun in a local waterpark. My thoughts drifted away and ended up reflecting on my past life. Accepting the Dubai project challenge was one of the few important experiences that cemented my career. But years before that event, another decision was even more crucial.

Do you remember the year 1999? Everyone was scared of the impending millennium bug and the internet and IT systems were still relatively undeveloped for mainstream use. Well, that was around the start of my IT career and I desperately wanted to be part of an SAP project. Mainly because it was a very desirable skill with promising longevity. At the time I was just a young inexperienced consultant, but my persistence earned me an opportunity. My first day as an SAP consultant was memorable, but more about that later.

I consider myself lucky that I am still earning my income directly related to SAP. The clothes I wear, the car I drive, the place I call home, all of them were possible thanks to SAP. And I am not the only one. Thousands of freelancers are dependent upon SAP as well. So it's not a surprise that this book focuses on SAP. That, and the fact that it is the worldwide market leader in offering an ERP solution to multinational companies. Many of the people who are financially dependent on SAP's success do not even know its history. That is why this chapter will be interesting for even the most experienced SAP consultants.

In 1972, the same year 'The Godfather' won an Oscar for Best Picture, four German ex-IBM colleagues founded SAP. Its abbreviation stands for 'Systemanalyse und Programmentwicklung' (System Analysis and Program Development). They introduced R/1, a financial accounting software solution. In those days, desktop computers or laptops did not exist. The displays needed to be connected to one single machine, called a 'mainframe computer'. The screen was text-based and offered only one colour; normally either orange or green.

Building on their initial success, the second release, R/2, followed a decade later. As Michael Jackson rose to dizzying heights of stardom with his 'Thriller' album, SAP clients were able to upgrade their financial SAP system to R/2 and experience the power of ERP for the first time. The functionality was spread over various modules, allowing clients to pick and choose what they wanted. Some only connected their accounting to sales and distribution, where others were mainly interested in manufacturing. But the more modules, the better the ERP experience.

Graphic design capabilities became more important during the 1990's, triggering the opportunity to redesign the ERP solution. By the time the European Union was founded with the signing of the Maastricht Treaty and twenty years after SAP's conception, the third release, R/3, saw the light of day. This was a much friendlier user interface, and the functionality expanded to offer a mature ERP solution.

Early in the new millennium, SAP wanted to step away from the modular approach. Instead they wanted to emphasise end-to-end business processes, many of them using a wide rage of modules.

Register to Report (RTR) encapsulates accounting.

Procure to Pay (PTP) emphasises logistics related to procurement.

Order to Cash (OTC) focuses on logistics associated to sales.

As expected, SAP removed the possibility to pay a licence for single modules. Almost overnight and without prior warning, a release upgrade turned R/3 into 'Enterprise Central Component' (ECC). This happened in the year 2006, when Nintendo introduced their revolutionary Wii console. Even though that is a long time ago, many consultants and recruiters still refer to these ancient R/3 modules. These days, you will limit yourself if you advertise your expertise as a module expert. You need to be able to master RTR, PTP and OTC to be considered a leading expert.

However, the modifications and evolution of the SAP ERP system didn't stop there. In 2015, the year Google put the first driverless cars on public roads, SAP started to rebuild their entire ERP solution from the ground up. They called it S/4, referring to the fourth release of their business suite. This time SAP ERP had become integrated with a dedicated SAP hardware solution, referred to as the 'High-Performance Analytic Appliance' (HANA). The primary objective is to speed up performance dramatically. Whereas a complex calculation took ECC several hours to complete, S/4 with HANA could do it in a matter of seconds.

Why am I providing all this technical context? Because when this book mentions SAP, it actually refers to their ECC or S/4 products.

Since my Dubai adventure, I have seen many clients struggle to implement SAP ERP. On almost every occasion more money was pumped into the project. In rare circumstances, the plug was pulled and millions of pounds disappeared into a black hole. Often the decision was made to start again with a clean sheet in the hope that this time the result would be better. As you can probably imagine, this is an entrepreneur's worst nightmare.

But now, you have access to the **Fast Implementation Track™** and can make your project a success story.

PART TWO

3 FAST IMPLEMENTATION TRACK™ (F.I.T.)

One specific Thursday morning several years ago, I attended my quarterly Strategic Coach® workshop with over 40 business owners. In each workshop we get the chance to focus purely on our future goals. We create structure for our business ideas and processes during those days. It is part of a global network of successful entrepreneurs, following the insights from the business coach Dan Sullivan.

It's a major bonus that I get to spend time with other entrepreneurs. They lead extremely profitable businesses employing, on average, several dozens of people. They all face similar challenges, opportunities and frustrations to mine. Therefore, we are able to effectively brainstorm breakthroughs and provide feedback. This workshop presented the perfect opportunity to verify a theory that I had in my mind. A theory I had been mulling over for quite some time. That is what Dan does. He makes you consider all sorts of entrepreneurial questions and apply actions to your insights.

Successful entrepreneurs learn from their mistakes. There is no such thing as 'failure', only experiences. All great entrepreneurs have lost everything and picked themselves up. They do it once, learn from it, and nothing scares them after that.

I felt as though I needed some insight into how to avoid bankruptcy. My desire was to take my business to the next level and multiply my revenues on a consistent basis. Bankruptcy would set me back severely and it was something I had stared in the face already.

Over the years I have certainly made some costly miscalculations, avoiding bankruptcy several times by the skin of my teeth. But many in the workshop have been bankrupt in the past. As the workshops are a safe haven, everyone is open to sharing their personal stories. So I had this idea buzzing in my head that needed verification. This was the perfect opportunity to hear the experiences and views of this group.

The workshop was about to start when I asked for a moment of their attention. With the microphone in my right hand and a folded piece of paper in my left, I invited the entrepreneurs to take on a challenge. They were to guess which seven words I had written down. These words formed a sentence that revealed the secret of how to avoid bankruptcy. It was my theory, and I was curious to see if they would verify it. They all took on this challenge gladly. So I placed the paper in a corner of the room, telling them not to take a sneak peek.

Throughout the entire day I received dozens of post-it notes with thoughts from my group on how they would avoid bankruptcy. They were seeking approval, but I was displaying my poker face. At the end of the day, everyone was eager to know what I had written down. Slowly I walked to the corner and picked up the note. Then I finally revealed my sentence to the group.

"Always have enough money in the bank."
~Isard Haasakker

As expected, they all agreed it made perfect sense. Every entrepreneur understands that incoming cash flow prevents bankruptcy, because it allows you to pay your bills. The customer invoice represents the healthiest source of income. That is considered common sense in business. Rob, my local electrician who runs his business from Fleet, instantly and wholeheartedly agrees. As does Colin, my hairdresser who owns a successful salon franchise in Kingston Upon Thames. But it is not common knowledge for those who don't run their own business. it is simply not something that they have to consider in order to do their jobs and live their lives successfully.

The payment receipt of a customer invoice is the most important event in your business. It prevents bankruptcy, keeping employees employed.
~Isard Haasakker

One day, I paid a visit to an Italian manufacturing site. Lorenzo, the head of the finance department, escorted me to a restaurant for lunch. He was a memorable chap. Classically Italian, I thought. Always perfectly dressed with a natural charisma that seemed to emanate success and happiness. He oozed confidence and a sort of artistic eccentricity that was hard not to like. Or to forget! Anyway, the story my quirky companion told me was heavy with irony and I couldn't help but feel for him. That said, the moral is to focus on what is important from the outset; cash flow.

Lorenzo's company had a portfolio of clients who were always extremely late with their payments. Sometimes it took twice as long as the agreed terms of payment! Even though everyone seemed to pay late, Lorenzo wanted to set a good example and provide exceptional service. He saw an opportunity to stand out amongst their competitors with a reputation for reliability. He always ensured that his suppliers were paid on time and in full.

This month however, he was not able to meet their financial obligations. So he went to the local bank and asked them for a short term loan. To his surprise, the bank declined. The rules around lending money were strict because businesses in that area were known for not paying on time or in full. Whatever Lorenzo argued, it didn't make a difference to the bank's verdict. In the end he was forced to postpone payments to his suppliers, forcing to become as unreliable as his own clients.

It just didn't sound fair! While the butterfly effect (localised change has a large effect elsewhere) described above is macrocosmic and affects multiple companies on an economic scale, scenarios of this nature are common and can happen on varying scales of destruction. As entrepreneurs are not involved in the daily activities of their multi-million pound projects, they are very dependent upon managers to keep an eye on deploying their vision.

When the project does not deliver results on time and in full, it becomes a difficult mission for the managers to plea for more money to complete the job. When the project gets derailed, it is interesting to observe the employees. Many are just expecting that additional funding is awarded. They do not feel the pain associated with rearranging pockets of money to keep the project afloat. Everything at their level just seems to be business as usual.

Occasionally, steering committee representatives make their appearance during regular team meetings to express that "'we need operate as a team" and "we need to help each other". Unfortunately, these monologues have little or no impact on those doing the daily work because they never see these senior managers and leaders outside of sporadic events. There is no personal connection. The message is meaningless and doesn't hit home. That is a shame to say the least because for team members, face time with upper management is an all too rare opportunity to try to understand the sense of urgency linked to these types of projects.

Instead, it would be very beneficial when upper management is engaged with the progress made within the project. As from day one their existence needs to be noticed. And their message needs to remain consistent. They can use the core **Fast Implementation Track™** components as a guide to make sure everyone is pointing in the right direction.

1. FOCUS on implementing business processes directly linked to the receipt of a customer payment.
2. COMMUNICATE what is on your mind, especially when it seems to be common sense.
3. SIMPLIFY your processes and procedures, using best practice available via standard functionality.
4. COMMIT and make the desired result a reality, by embracing change.
5. EDUCATE everyone, to enable them to contribute.

It is extremely valuable for everyone to be able to tap into the mind of the successful entrepreneur. Avoiding bankruptcy is high on their agenda. That explains why successful multinational companies keep an enormous amount of cash on their books. It is a survival strategy. That's why we sometimes sense the reluctance of upper management to spend this money unnecessarily. Implementing SAP ERP easily costs millions of pounds. Risk mitigation is key. That is why everyone needs to understand and embrace the **Fast Implementation Track™**.

Knowing and following the insights provided by these five simple components of the **Fast Implementation Track™** is everyone's responsibility. Luckily, they are highlighted in more details throughout the next chapters.

4 FOCUS

Let me take you back to Dubai once more. If you remember, I was flown out there for two month go-live support after implementing SAP ERP functionality. We only had three months to get it all ready. The core team consisted of only two people, myself included. Due to extreme time pressures Peter, the director of the Dubai company, was very clear about his priorities. He needed to be able to legally purchase goods, store them and then sell them on to clients in the Middle East.

He was not looking for perfection. Instead, he was looking for progress in enabling the most basic of business processes. Due to the timescales involved, the only available option was to implement standard SAP. Everyone needed to be pragmatic when an existing business process would not fit that mould. As there was no time to change SAP, the business needed to change instead. That also applied to their suppliers and clients.

It can be quite difficult to estimate the cost of implementing SAP ERP. This book uses a relatively simple approach to allow you an indication of how quickly the project finances can get out of hand. Just for argument's sake, assume that the cost of implementation can be estimated by forecasting £1,000 per full time resource per day. This would include their salary or rate, but also various other costs like flights, accommodation, customer support, real estate rental, licence fees and computer hardware.

When implementing SAP within three months and with just two months go-live support by two people, the overall cost would be approximately £200,000.

But when you are part of a six year implementation in a team of 50 people, this quickly costs £60 million. This would mean postponing deployment by one additional month would cost a staggering additional £1 million.

During one specific implementation project, my colleagues had to deal with a particularly demanding individual who was representing the company for sales and marketing. You know, the one who you can always rely on to see the negative and get defensive over the smallest things. A moaner, always going to aggressive lengths to assume authority over others. Somehow the bosses always seem to like them.

Nicknames are inevitable for people like that. He was most peculiar. On the one hand he was smart; always dressed in a suit and tie, and freshly shaven. But what was going on with his socks?! They were always bright pink, green or yellow. They completely clashed with the sophisticated look of his blue, Saville Row suit. Whereas you or I might look stupid with such a contrasting appearance, on him it only seemed to compound his air of confidence. You almost didn't want to question him, such was his charisma. I used to wonder if loud socks were a deliberate tactic to assume control, or whether he simply didn't know they looked so out of place. We called him Mister Marvellous.

Let me give you an example of how this guy worked. Every time my team resolved one business requirement, a set of new ones seemed to surface almost immediately. It was always Mister Marvellous making the requests, never anyone else. We all noticed the pattern as time went by. The requests for change become ever weirder and unrealistic. Everyone wanted to call him out on his behaviour. We all felt he was wasting the team's time and the company's budget.

Unfortunately, he was the only one who knew the current system design. No-one felt they could challenge him to verify whether or not his wishes represented true requirements. And so he continued, becoming more outrageous and suspicious with each day that passed. It takes a lot of time and energy to keep on finding solutions to questionable requests. We were convinced that this man had a specific aim to discredit the new SAP ERP system. Either that or he was power-tripping.

Suffice to say, he wasn't a business owner. Had it been his own time and money, I'm sure he would have acted very differently. Just imagine for a minute that you lose focus in your organisation and allow all sorts of business processes and non-standard additional developments. It doesn't take a rocket scientist to figure out that the number of consultants required, as well as overall lead-time, would increase.

This can quickly cost a business millions.

Don't you wish we could have taken Mister Marvellous to visit Lorenzo, the amiable Italian introduced in the previous chapter? He could have quickly explained the impact of losing focus on what's important. If Mister Marvellous had the correct focus, it would have eliminated the need for me to join that project altogether. My project involvement lasted for six months. So using the assumed £1,000 per person per day rate, working 20 days each month, he would have been able to save the company £120,000. This is a cringe worthy price to pay for allowing your team to lose focus.

Losing focus is common and it seems to be linked to a tendency to over complicate business. It can take years to define a blueprint for a project. But it is actually surprisingly easy to list all your core processes.

The payment receipt of a customer invoice is the most important event in your business.
~Isard Haasakker

Simply focus on the payment receipt of a customer invoice as the central point of attention. Follow the flow of information, goods and money before and after this event. Just take a moment to assess your business. Here is a summary of the meeting with Peter that took place the afternoon after I agreed to join the team for the Dubai SAP ERP implementation project.

When you sell physical goods, you want to inform your client of a reliable delivery date when you receive their order. In most cases you keep sufficient goods in storage for immediate delivery. But sometimes you need to replenish from your supplier first. When there is a clear sense of urgency, you can ask your supplier to deliver directly to your client.

Mistakes can happen. So you need to have a return process in place to collect the goods from your client. Damaged stock is normally scrapped or returned to your supplier. But in some circumstances you can repair the damages, potentially outsourcing this activity by means of a subcontracting agreement.

When your company is not cash-rich, you can ask whether your supplier is willing to remain the owner of the goods they deliver. It is called vendor consignment. Ownership only changes when you register a sale. This type of agreement is also possible with your client, whereby you remain the owner until your client is able to pass it along themselves. That would be a customer consignment agreement.

Of course you can register each payment individually. Ideally you automate that process. Every night you can schedule bank transfers to your suppliers. At the same time, your client can authorise you to debit their bank account to pay the invoices.

You need to print documents to support your business processes. Apart from issuing billing documents, you can also send order confirmations to your clients.

You have to comply with legal reporting requirements. Everyone is allowed to view your Balance Sheet along with the Profit and Loss Statement. You want to make sure every month that this data is accurate and complete. That also assists in assessing how much Value Added Tax you have to pay.

Reliable internal profitability analysis would be important as well. You may decide to reserve a part of your turnover to estimate the cost for the transport of your goods. Then you estimate the monthly bill from your transportation service providers by recording the planned cost for each transport in a purchase order. When the final bill arrives, you settle the actual cost against the planned cost.

If you find it difficult to list the core business processes, simply use existing customer billing documents to trace the actions that happened within your organisation. Use the printed output to ask your employees to trace the information, goods and money flows. You would be amazed by the wealth of knowledge contained within your company. There could be a realisation that many of the processes and procedures do not add any value. That is a good opportunity to scrutinise your current activities and decide to discontinue or outsource them. That would immediately increase efficiency and productivity.

You'd be surprised at just how fast a knowledgeable SAP consultant is able to configure a working SAP ERP system. That includes all the vital business processes in accounting and logistics. This is made possible first and foremost by focusing on the payment receipt of the customer invoice. Other bells and whistles can follow at a later time.

5 COMMUNICATE

If you overheard someone complaining in a Chinese restaurant about the pieces of chicken in their chicken soup, would it astonish you? Or would you do the same?

My friend William told me an amusing tale of his recent visit to a Chinese restaurant. After a long day he treated himself on the way back to his hotel. As he perused the extensive menu, his eyes locked onto the chicken soup. He shut the menu and ordered quickly, looking forward to a steaming bowl of soothing home cooking. A taste of home away from home. The waitress wrote down his order and hurried off to the kitchen to pass the order to the chef. So far, so good. My friend waited patiently for his food.

Now, when you believe you have been clear about your instructions, it can be surprising to learn that they have been misinterpreted. Especially when you think you have asked for something obvious and straightforward, like a bowl of chicken soup. However, William was in for such a surprise. Remember, he was in a Chinese restaurant.

There is a twist to this tale and if you haven't got it yet, you have been caught by 'syntax ambiguity'; a situation where a sentence or statement can be interpreted in more than one way due to its ambiguous structure. Syntax ambiguity happens all the time at work. It'll be costing your company a fortune. It is often the reason projects are delayed, or worse, not delivered at all. There are plenty of horror stories of expensive initiatives that are shelved after several years and it is almost always down to ambiguity and a lack of thorough two-way communication. Whenever I see one of those ambiguous headlines, I always think of the millions of pounds that have been flushed down the drain.

In the past, I have worked at many companies who have expedited their development off-shore. This immediately triggers the need to manage cultural differences. There are many examples where the East (Asia) clashes with the West (Europe and North America). Let me share some with you.

For starters, in the West people tend to be focused on their own personal goals. That is quite in contrast to the East, where the success of your team is far more important. In the West you try to be direct and clear with the instructions you communicate to others. In the East, the focus is more on providing suggestions and subtle clues. Imagine the difference between, "do not drive when it is icy outside", and "there is a lot of snow on the road this morning". Both statements aim to communicate the same warning. But the latter is much more subtle and the suggested action might not come across.

It probably doesn't surprise you that there are differences in the way the East and West deal with authority. In the West, it is acceptable to question statements made by your manager. In the East, you have to be careful not to intimidate your superior, especially within companies still embracing a more traditional culture.

But here is the real killer.

Managers in the West consider themselves to be a part of the team. In the East, hierarchical structures can be taken literally. Whereas in the West a manager welcomes constructive feedback, in the East, managers often do not receive feedback at all. Now contemplate what happens when colleagues in the East are offered work by managers in the West. Can you imagine the barriers a difference in culture create? Communication can get distorted as a consequence. Just like William is about to discover, having ordered chicken soup.

So my friend was in the Chinese restaurant and he was getting really hungry. He was starting to wonder how long it can possibly take to make a bowl of chicken soup. Just as he was debating whether or not to ask after its whereabouts, the waitress appeared again with a hot bowl and walked directly towards his table. As she placed the bowl down, William picked up his spoon and was about to dig in when he noticed the pieces of chicken in the soup. A far cry from the succulent, meaty chunks his mother had always added when he was ill as a child. Instead, he was looking down upon a floating chicken head and feet! And of course when he asked why it was in there, he was met with an equal look of confusion and irritation. But what did he expect when ordering a bowl of chicken soup from a restaurant in rural China?!

The syntax ambiguity I deliberately used when I set this scene meant that you probably thought William was in a Chinese restaurant somewhere in the UK, and not in a restaurant in China, as was indeed the reality. The chicken soup story creates awareness that a simple request can lead to unexpected results. Communication is not as easy as it may initially seem. It is always vital to verify whether or not the message is clearly understood. So after you've identified an issue, what next?

Let me start by emphasising that a clear definition of the problem is vital. Before diving into any detail with the recipients of your communication, you must provide clarity to everyone else by naming the issue. Highlight the purpose of resolving it and the importance of this to everyone and the business. Questions such as, "How does this problem affect the client, supplier and employee?" and "What is the impact on market shares and profit margins when the problem does not get resolved?" should be answered in a way that everyone understands clearly. Make sure you empathise with the people affected, for it is their disappointment, frustration and anguish that may need to be managed.

Once you have emotionally diffused the situation and eliminated the need for anyone to get upset or defensive, you can work to find the most suitable solution. Bring everyone involved and available together in a group and offer them all the definition of the problem. Give them some time to reflect, without discussion, on what did work about the circumstances surrounding the issue and what didn't. This will trigger what I call a 'mindstorm'. Then, come together and share the ideas during a 'brainstorm'.

Each solution has to be noted even if it sounds unrealistic, and everyone must be able to join in. This can be hard when there are different characters in a group. Some are louder than others. Some take longer than others. Some have more ideas than others. The key is to put a sensible timeframe around the session and ask everyone for their input.

At this point the focus is on teamwork and creativity. No one should be concerned with how a suggestion will be implemented as this can encourage premature negation of a viable solution that just needs some further thought. They just need to think freely in order to come up with creative solutions. For effective brainstorming, how something will work in reality is not important. Avoid dampening creative thought processes by saying things like, "I can't see how that's going to work". When the group is mid-flow, you could be limiting the potential of the group to find the best solution. How it will work in practice is what will be determined once the brainstorm is complete.

As a group you can decide which solutions are worth investigating in more detail. Make a shortlist of your favourite ideas. List the *Strengths*, *Weaknesses*, *Opportunities* and *Threats* of each idea into a SWOT analysis. Then debate which solution makes the most sense to investigate further in more detail.

Now here is the trick many people forget.

To avoid running around in circles, it is important to document the results of the SWOT analysis. If the available options are not recorded, the road towards a preferred solution gets blocked. After a while, even the people involved forget which options were on the table. This simply allows dominant personalities to overrule others. A perfect opportunity to confuse and rule.

Imagine how quickly the argumentation to select the final solution is forgotten as well. It can be effective to vote in a shortlist of the top three ideas. Then allow the more analytical and detail orientated group members sufficient time to research their feasibility. Upon return they present to the whole group for a final vote on the best option. You also need to note why the other solutions were not selected.

Let me quickly recap:
- Make the problem meaningful.
- Mindstorm before a brainstorm.
- SWOT the potential solutions.
- Document the decisions made.

If it is not written down, it never happened.

Imagine you have decided on a way forward to solve the problem. The most crucial follow-up document is one that describes how you are going to test the expected results. Error-handling often gets neglected or even ignored, which is a monumental mistake. As soon as you design the solution, you need to be able to foresee any obstacles and define strategies to circumnavigate them.

Every single mishap needs to be identified and clarified. The more eye for detail, the more likely that the solution will be robust. As you're in business, you probably know Murphy's Law. It states that anything that can go wrong, will go wrong. This isn't negativity. It is foresight. It would be negativity if the solution was already underway and then someone points out mistakes and starts complaining. In the strategizing phase though, it's not only diligent but absolutely necessary to pick the desired result apart and reassemble it with good ideas that act as joints.

There is one more thing that needs your attention. I cannot recommend it enough. It is something I've addressed from the outset in the book. When communicating your vision and leading team brainstorming sessions, make sure you are jargon-busting all the way. Every company uses their own 'lingo' and this needs to be explained in layman's terms. Literally defined, a layman is someone who needs a satisfying explanation for everything because they don't have any specialised knowledge in any particular area.

Imagine a child who is constantly asking, "Why". Keep on answering the why question until everything is clear. A large number of team members do not dare to ask for an explanation of jargon. That is irrespective of whether they live in the East or West. Much like they won't ask for clarity on the company's vision, or question a leader as to why they're doing certain things in a certain way.

It's a shame, but an awful lot of people, employees in particular, would not dare to question why their chicken soup contains head and feet, rather than the expected succulent pieces of meat. They just don't want to rustle any feathers. Just because nobody is questioning the quality and effectiveness of communication, it does not mean that there is nothing to worry about. In fact, the opposite is likely to be true.

Imagine you explain something to a group of people that is not within their normal frame of reference. Afterwards you ask, "Are there any questions?". When there is no response, does that mean everybody understood your message?

Let me take you back when I first started as a junior business consultant. There was an impromptu team meeting during which someone made reference to the Fortune 500. I had no idea what that meant. So I raised my hand and asked for clarification. Some of my colleagues laughed, as if it was something that was common knowledge. To add insult to injury, my question was not answered. I searched on the Internet to discover that it represents the largest corporations within the United States of America at a given moment in time.

Several days later at lunchtime, other team members confided with me that they also wanted to ask about the Fortune 500 but they'd been too embarrassed to say anything. And thanks to me, they were glad they didn't. Needless to say, there was a culture in which honest curiosity was ridiculed. If you're a leader, lead by example. Make sure you create an environment whereby the only stupid question is the question not asked.

Anymore questions? No? Thought so. Let's move on.

The thought patterns of an entrepreneur can be alien to those who design the ERP system so it's crucial to communicate your vision to the entire team. Make it clear that the payment of a customer invoice triggers incoming cash flow. This reduces the risk of bankruptcy and job losses. Everyone should be aware that bells and whistles are not vital for a successful ERP implementation.

In my experience, it is extremely rare that upper management get involved in expressing their vision. A real chance for project consultants to contact any member of the project steering committee directly is occasional at best. Even though they provide the multi million pound investment, their expectations and concerns will not reach the work floor.

If the entrepreneur, CEO or CIO has a clear vision, they must communicate that to all departments. Then everyone can work together to ensure that the customer invoice payment is prominent in your daily business. Your involvement to enable that vital business event gives you clarity on your importance within the company. That in turn ignites job satisfaction. A great achievement when you successfully communicate your focus.

When you assume, assume that you assume wrong.
~Isard Haasakker

6 SIMPLIFY

A few years ago I was supporting a data migration project. We were getting close to the weekend prior to go-live and all was going swimmingly. On day, out of the blue, a problem emerged. As it appeared, the legacy system allows the sales price in Pound Sterling to be stored up to five decimals. There was a fear that this would not be possible in SAP. A meeting was swiftly arranged and I was representing the project team. What happened during that meeting amazed me.

Yes, it is true that SAP stores prices up to two decimals in Pound Sterling. But you can easily convert a £0.12345 unit price into £123.45 per 1,000 pieces. Maybe I was a bit too indifferent about it. But other people in the room were not easily convinced. Their main fear related to users making mistakes when maintaining prices. In other words, there was a consensus that they employ people who might not be able to understand the solution I was offering.

This started a long and exhausting analysis process.

Somehow the project manager was instructed by the stakeholders to find another solution. Many more meetings followed, involving even more managers who needed to get their voice heard. It basically got out of control. Probably the most interesting request was to calculate the potential loss in turnover when you rounded down the unit price from five decimals to two decimals. Mind you, this related to products with a low value but high sales volume.

Rounding down £0.12345 to £0.12 for a product that sold over a million times each year resulted in a loss of at least £3,450. In itself, this was not staggering but there were thousands of products that could be affected. So applying this approach costed the company millions in turnover. Obviously, this was not appeasing the upper management who also got involved eventually. Their first reaction was to suggest renegotiating some of the prices using commercial rounding. This way, they figured they could recuperate potential losses and eliminate the problem. But then you need to renegotiate the price lists with your clients. You can imagine the sales representatives felt that this was going to be tough.

It is weird how easily you can get sucked into seeking a complex solution to fix a simple problem. The obvious way out was staring straight at us. We were just too busy not to notice it. Suddenly the answer fell into my head while jogging through the forest on a Sunday morning. What if we were to add a simple check to avoid human error? It all fell into place. You could link the sales price with the cost price. When we needed to maintain the sales price up to five decimals, then we could also register the cost price with five decimals.

Luckily these products were already clearly identifiable as they were reported using specific material groups. So when a product belonged to a specific material group, we could ensure that the cost and sales prices were maintained per 1,000 pieces. My enthusiasm was initially curbed by my colleagues but eventually I was able to persuade everyone to take this approach. These checks were implemented quickly and we could lay this issue to rest.

While everyone swiftly paid attention to other calamities, I took some time to reflect on this experience. The agreed solution would only take a few days to implement but first, countless, expensive managers were involved, requesting others to do various types of investigations. Converting time into cash made me realise that it costed the company at least £25,000. They could have done many other things with this wasted time and money. And people wonder why ERP projects get delayed.

There are clear benefits to sticking with the standard SAP functionality. Any defects in standard functionality will be resolved by SAP free of charge. New functionality can be easily incorporated into the existing processes and procedures. The cost for a release upgrade will be minimal too, as you do not need to test whether standard functionality still works in the latest version. So the closer to standard functionality you go, the easier it is to take full advantage of new trends in your business or industry.

The relative ease and flexibility of standard SAP really came to light during my time in Dubai. Given just three months to implement a fully functioning ERP system, there was simply no time to discuss deviations. We just had to make it happen with the available standard functionality. And we did. The company was able to trade normally from the very first day. They could collect payments from clients and pay their suppliers. While they continued to do business, they also put money aside to fund any enhancements that showed a promising return on investment. That is the smart way to introduce ERP into your business.

Don't get me wrong. If anyone had said to me on that plane journey home, "it's just standard SAP functionality, it's a piece of cake!", I would have had to restrain myself from saying something I might later regret! It was a big push to get it done in three months. But the point is that it is the most effective route to implementation. It also provides the most immediate benefits to you and your business.

Now that I have the whole process documented and refined, it is actually possible to achieve this in a far shorter time frame.

It is often the case that your employees copy functionality in their current system to fit into SAP. We can all understand why this might happen. It appears to be the easiest approach. They think it will be easier to mould SAP to their current way of working than the other way around. However, the consultants involved should then point out that SAP only became the worldwide market leader by offering best practice as standard.

Simplify to multiply.   ~Dan Sullivan

Actually, many consultants are not aware of what can be achieved with standard SAP. They fail to challenge the business requirements written by those lacking any SAP experience. Lateral thinking is thrown out of the window. Too often, too quickly, consultants suggest businesses to deviate from standard functionality unnecessarily. Even when simple change management activities could avoid a costly redesign. They can't keep it simple, as they do not know the standard.

Dan Sullivan, Founder of Strategic Coach®, says that you need to simplify in order to multiply. Even though entrepreneurs typically agree with this statement, those executing their vision often do not see the long term benefits of this approach. Managers and consultants tend to make decisions based on the known past and present. Entrepreneurs look several years ahead. Once you are clear on your goals to multiply your business, you can work backwards from that vision to pin-point the necessary backstage systems and processes which underlie the day to day running of your business.

These systems and processes are ultimately the support structure for your bigger vision. They need to be simplified to ensure your business runs like a well-oiled machine, and grows at the right pace. This is why strong change management (e.g. focus and communication) needs to come into play when simplifying the ERP solution by embracing standard functionality.

We also have to realise that enhancements to the standard are likely to be required. Before you go ahead and alter the standard, use a simple method to verify whether changes are really necessary. Over the years I've compiled a list of reasons to deviate from standard SAP. This book contains a fragment of my **Enhancement Approval Checklist™**:

- Data migration and data governance.
- Document generation and distribution.
- Legal requirements not supported in the standard system.
- Your unique selling point is not identified as global best practice.
- Automating steps within a process.
- Implementing business requirements from your biggest client.

Data migration and Data Governance.

Normally, you would need to transfer a lot of data from your legacy systems such as clients, suppliers, products, prices, outstanding orders and payments. That would require tailor-made developments during the implementation. Ideally, you want to ensure that the quality of this data is guaranteed afterwards by defining rules for governance. The smart approach is to recycle developments made during data migration to support data governance. Only this doesn't happen very often. Governance gets neglected, costing your company millions in the near future. Alternatively, a separate costly project is initiated to reinvent the wheel to ensure proper data governance.

Let's return to my example of the sales price in Pound Sterling using five decimals. This was a topic for the data migration team to resolve. However, the agreed solution also included checks in the system after migration. When the cost price was defined per 1,000 pieces, then the sales price also needed to be per 1,000 pieces. This is a typical governance related validation. This validation rule was developed as part of data migration, but reused afterwards to support data governance.

Document generation and distribution.

In all honesty, the standard SAP document layouts are not that great. It makes sense to design your own. At the same time, it would be useful to introduce the ability to convert this output into PDF, archive them and distribute by email. All these actions require additions to the SAP standard.

It is very common that the customer invoice is accompanied with transportation details. Many companies prefer to include which invoiced products are in which container, along with the dimensions and weight. Various tracking numbers may also be printed. This level of detail is not a legal requirement. Therefore, SAP does not offer this in their standard billing layouts.

Legal requirements not supported in the standard system.

Some country-specific legal requirements have not been included in the standard SAP functionality. At the moment of writing this book, Greek domestic billing is a good example. Various legal requirements exist to allow the Greek government to audit goods movements along with their financial consequences. This audit control is enforced by associating every delivery and billing document with a government-specific reference number. That allows the government to verify whether or not the goods have been moved between the buyer and seller, and whether a payment has been issued and paid. In addition, a tax spooler machine is used to issue a unique number printed on each legal document and to keep track of the details mentioned in each document.

The Greek government has been using a specific code book with all the procedures that Greek companies should follow when they trade within Greece. This specific codebook is used to allow the Greek government to control businesses and audit them. If companies are not running according to this specific codebook, legal issues could arise, resulting in huge financial penalties or even revoking the license to trade within Greece.

As a result, the Greek subsidiary of SAP offers all the relevant reports and outputs, also referred to as Greek localization or Hellenization. Still, when you trade within Greece, you quickly need to build additional developments to make it all work properly.

Your unique selling point is not identified as global best practice.

Imagine you have a process uniquely designed to attract clients away from your competition. However, the procedures and processes are not fully covered within the standard SAP functionality. If no other software company is offering a suitable resolution that fits within SAP, it would make sense to develop your own solution.

If your business is operating in the Fast Moving Consumer Goods (FMCG) market, you might have heard of *Fill Or Kill* during sales order processing. When your client places an order, they have an expectation that the demand can be met instantly. When insufficient stock is available, you should not keep this demand in the system as a backorder. So either you fill the demand, or you kill it. It might surprise you that this process is not covered within standard SAP. Instead you would have to build your own solution to offer this service to your clients.

Automating steps within a process.

Some processes require several people to perform specific tasks in the SAP system. When these are repetitive and never change, you could decide to automate them. That would also speed up the entire process and eliminate the potential human error at the same time. A good example is the integration between sales and procurement. When a customer sale triggers procurement, then you can arrange the purchase order to be created without the need for human intervention. A similar solution is often implemented when a sale triggers specific activities within your warehouse.

Implementing business requirements from your biggest client.

You might want to offer special services to your most loyal clients who generate a significant turnover. Losing their business would seriously impact the profitability of your business. In the past I worked on a project where one sole customer was directly linked to 70% of all business transactions. And that client was well aware of that fact. It would not surprise you that very specific business requirements were enforced.

Normally customer billing is triggered when the goods leave the warehouse. However, this strategically vital client would prefer billing after the goods have been received. You use a *Proof Of Delivery* as the basis for billing. However, you would need to enhance the system when you only want to offer this *Proof Of Delivery* option for strategic clients.

In those circumstances it makes sense to implement this functionality as if it were available for any customer. It would give you the opportunity to offer *Proof of Delivery* billing as a reward when ad-hoc customers become loyal clients.

Whatever the reason to deviate from the standard functionality, remember that time is money. Keeping an eye on the core vision expressed in this book is important. The payment receipt of a customer invoice is essential for your business survival. Any functionality not related in any shape or form to a customer payment should be scrutinised. If the standard offering does not meet your needs, then use the **Enhancement Approval Checklist™** as a guide to decide to build your own solution.

You can only multiply when you simplify. Simplification allows your business to work as a well-oiled machine based on clearly defined repetitive processes. Any other approach is inviting unnecessary complexity into your business. That consumes time and money and drives you away from your focus on what matters the most. True growth comes with simplification as it is easier to replicate. With this approach, SAP ERP implementations are more likely to deploy on time and within budget.

7 COMMIT

I once had the pleasure of working with an interesting guy who made quite an impact on me and really made me think about the importance of commitment. He had a colourful background and a larger than life presence. You always knew when he was in the building. He would sweep through the office with imperial energy, talk louder than anyone else in the room, and make decisions after asking only a few questions. He would be certain his was the right decision and would never change his mind afterwards. He is the sort of person who would be the life and soul of the party and has somehow managed to find a way to be his own self and win, whatever the situation. He was truly unique, I thought.

My friend here was not only heavily involved in the new system implementation, he had also been awarded control of the transition for the sales and marketing processes. The business believed someone had to know all of the moving parts in order to prescribe the necessary system functionality. He was also instrumental in deciding which system would be the best fit in the first place, and the steering committee identified him as the only one with the intellect and gravitas to get the job done.

It is true that there needs to be knowledge of all the moving parts of your SAP project, and we've covered that earlier in this book. But my advice relates to the entire team, not just to one person holding all the cards. Most importantly, this guy was an external consultant. That gave him an enormous bargaining power. He made sure that his knowledge was not documented. It was all his own 'expertise'. Decisions were made based on what he thought at any given time. So he had access to all of the business' intellectual property, even though the business had no record of his. The company became even more dependent upon his services.

He was under no contractual obligation to stay longer than agreed. If he were to end his contract today, how would everyone else be able to pick up from where he left off? The company had put themselves in danger of going back to square one, and having to bring in someone else to learn and document all of the sales and marketing processes and oversee implementation. This would immediately endanger the planned deployment date of the SAP ERP project, potentially costing the business a fortune.

When SAP was decided as the new ERP tool, they appointed him an assistant. Sarah had just graduated from university and was eager to learn as much as she could about SAP. Over time, it became clear that he was making up business requirements for the sake of it. The requests became more outrageous with every week that passed. Does he sound familiar yet? Yes, I am referring to Mister Marvellous. So impressive at first, but left chaos in his wake. Of course, he was laughing all the way to the bank whilst the company had to pay for his messes. Sarah was too inexperienced to challenge him. Besides, she was only focusing on how these issues could be solved within SAP to build up her own knowledge-base.

You could say that the company made the wrong type of commitment. Sure, in the beginning there may well have been good intentions but in the end you are running a business. And that also includes the assurance that key people can be replaced at any given time without jeopardising the daily business. Instead companies gladly outsource their vital business knowledge without thinking of the repercussions. During this SAP ERP project, Mister Marvellous was clearly resisting change, most likely because change was not in his personal interests. He feared that his current knowledge would become obsolete. Because of his superiority, the company was fearing change rather than embracing it.

Jason Clarke has an interesting TED talk on change management. As well as talking about change in relation to taking a passion and making it a reality, he knows that people are, by definition, afraid of change. He cleverly asserts that in most cases a refusal is not a real argument.

When someone tells you that "it has always been like this", then he really lets you know the problem is much older than you think.

Others could argue that "it is the same everywhere", meaning the problem is much wider than you think.

You might hear, "It is not in the budget", only highlighting that the money was spent on the wrong things.

Or you get the response that, "It is not in our charter", indirectly signalling that the people who came up with the vision weren't thinking as big as you are.

And you have the famous quote that, "It's political", providing insight that they have learnt to keep their ideas to themselves.

Finally, it is often said "It is traditional", admitting that they don't know why they do the things they do.

How do you react when you hear these clichés? Jason Clarke reassures that the comebacks to these false arguments are easy.

Imagine you are working alongside a consultant who believes that change is too complicated. You can react by saying, "That's alright, let me simplify it for you".

If you are confronted by a manager who kindly reminds you that innovation is not in your job description, and that, "It's not what we pay you for", simply reply that your idea came free of charge.

Jason observes the most common reasons to resist change and how to battle them.

I'm too full of emotion and fear to think about this.

They are probably in a negative state of mind. Let them talk about their emotions. Ask them how they feel and why they think they feel that way. Be mindful not to criticise or become defensive. This isn't personal or a sign they don't value their job. Just let them express their feelings. Eventually, when all the negativity has been exhausted, allow them to see the light at the end of the tunnel.

Let them know you understand and you're sorry they feel that way. Explain that you are feeling motivated because when you look at this change, you see a bigger future and exciting developments. Soon, they will see the positive effects that comes with change. In the meantime, you only have to listen to them. New information can come as a huge shock to some people.

When you hear this sentence, you know they are just processing the information. Just like when a child falls down and looks at the reaction of the people surrounding it. Working out whether to laugh or cry, your calmness and understanding is the perfect non-verbal communication to take away any sense of fear.

I'm scared of the transition, not the idea.

Their current situation is known, structured, proven, certain and reassuring. It's safe and by suggesting change, a fear of the unknown and discomfort kicks in. It is not your idea this person is rejecting; it is the journey to the idea. During the transition to get from A to B you need to control failure, loss, rejection, ridicule, risk, fear, anxiety, confusion, waste, blame, shame, pain and exhaustion. When you keep everyone up to date during the transition, then you can eliminate the impact of these roadblocks during the transition phase.

I don't know how big a deal this change really is.

This kind of resistance can be resolved by doing a simple exercise.

First, list all the things that will remain the same. Then highlight all the things you still cannot do. These two lists reflect business as usual.

Follow up with a list of what would not be possible anymore. We all have to understand why scrapping this functionality is necessary. Then we must accept this will happen. In most cases they are sacrifices to simplify your business in order to multiply in the near future.

Finally, show what new exciting things will become possible. This final list should make anyone excited to commit to change.

I feel like I have no say in what happens.

Often change is forced upon people. That doesn't work. Instead, make people part of the design for change. When they have the ability to influence change, they will become invested in making a change for the better. This also comes back to communication. When business leaders communicate openly their vision and the direction the company will go in over the next 6-12 months, team members are able to actively engage with it. While some people succumb to fear, as discussed above, others will rise to the occasion and start innovating in their roles to make further progress.

I'm fed up with phoney change that goes nowhere.

People are actually not resisting change when they say this. What they want is real change. A change for the better. They know when change is just a repackaged old idea. Most people learn how to stay out of trouble, and not to rustle any feathers. Still, they want to be part of a change that makes an impact. Real change impacts the way we think. Real change will become a success when everyone involved is invited to become an influencing part of it.

Change management plays a vital part in all of this. But it only works when you assign managers who have the capability to focus, communicate without ambiguity, and apply a strategy to implement simplicity. But above all, persuade everyone to embrace *real change*. When a team is passionate about a shared goal and they all have a stake in it, commitment will follow.

SAP is able to offer so many exciting possibilities to your business. When people feel that they can contribute to making a final difference, they're encouraged to focus on results. Make sure they are recognised for their hard work. You will instantly see their commitment to the project and to your business shoot through the roof.

8 EDUCATE

You might remember Sarah, Mister Marvellous' plucky graduate assistant. As a brief reminder, she was a recent graduate with limited knowledge of SAP but a burning desire to learn, and had to deal with the freelance consultant who made us think he didn't really want SAP to be deployed. He resisted the change he couldn't control and seemed incentivised by nothing more than his own pay check. In the meantime, Sarah sensed at an early stage that she would have to hold the fort when he decided to leave, or was kicked out.

Instead of being overwhelmed by the idea, Sarah stepped into the trenches and got to work. She put together a plan, secretly collecting and documenting everything he knew. She soaked up all the information she possibly could, irrespective of the source, like a sponge. She was a quick learner, understanding the solutions solving the outrageous requirements issued by Mister Marvellous. Her progress did not go unnoticed.

Only a few weeks after the SAP ERP deployment, rumours started to emerge about Mister Marvellous. People wondered why he was working from home, something he never used to do. At the same time Sarah was radiating more confidence than ever before.

Then an email was sent out to everyone. Sarah was taking over from Mister Marvellous. We never saw him again. That was the fastest and most dramatic promotion I have ever witnessed. Good for her. She deserved it.

Education is really about leaving your comfort zone and showing your commitment to the end result. Being hungry to know more and getting comfortable with being in a constant state of learning is the key to success and happiness. Sarah is the perfect example.

It takes me back to my first day as a SAP consultant.

I'll never forget that feeling. I was both excited and nervous but eager to get started and get to grips with SAP, which was making waves in the industry at that time. A man took me to the room that would be my home for the next few months. My new desk had a shiny new desktop computer and the display showed that they logged me into the SAP system. Then he left. I waited patiently for him to come back. Hoping he probably just gone to get some training materials. Half an hour later, I was still sitting there and no-one had returned.

Confused, I poked my head out the office door which looked out onto the main floor. It was a large company and I knew I'd landed a big deal in working there, especially on my first job. The room outside my little office was hectic, to say the least. The phones were ringing, people were rushing backwards and forwards with folders and papers in their hands. No-one was making eye contact. Two executive-types spilled out of a board room loudly and shook hands. Everyone seemed so busy!

Through fear of being noticed, I popped my head quickly back inside my room and shut the door quietly. Slowly I sat behind my desk and stared at the SAP screen. Where to start? This system was alien to me. Time to panic.

The door opened and two people walked into the room. They took seats at the other two desks having introducing themselves. Janet and Steve gave me all the time I needed to learn the SAP system. They made sure I was able to complete my deliverables on time, sacrificing their busy schedule. They saved my bacon, and taught me the importance of teamwork.

Several years later, when I was offered the opportunity to configure logistics within seemingly impossible timeframes for that company in Dubai, I wondered why they had asked me to be part of this rapid implementation. Weeks later I found out that they had asked more senior consultants. They'd all declined. Maybe Peter came all the way from Dubai to ensure that I would be persuaded to join the team. That would explain why they ushered me into the position without much explanation.

When I reminisce on my first day as an SAP consultant, I notice how much progress I have made since then. Understanding the difference a great team of people can make. Like Sarah, I discovered the importance of learning new capabilities quickly. That, I decided, was as good a building block as any. Maybe that was the reason why I accepted the Dubai challenge. Just say, "Yes" and have the conviction that you will figure it out while you go along. Trust yourself.

Dramatically widening your comfort zone within an extremely short timespan should be seen as an exciting challenge. You will discover that you can do miracles when you put your mind and energy to it. The truth is, I haven't been afraid of change since Janet and Steve entered that small room. From that moment, I've constantly aimed to widen my comfort zone and share my knowledge to anyone who wants to listen.

As a rule, I accept new contract opportunities based on the challenge and the opportunity to learn new skills. This keeps me relevant in the market place and I firmly believe it is an attitude everyone should apply.

Sadly, it is not common for businesses to invest in education. So much so that most businesses don't even include it in the budget. Either you learn on the job or sacrifice your own spare time. This is a travesty. Failing to recognise the great importance of education within your own organisation can be the difference between success or failure.

When it comes to SAP ERP, the comfort zone can be approached via two different angles: *functionality* and *capability*.

From a functionality perspective, the traditional SAP R/3 modules are still used as a reference to identify someone's knowledge of the system. Those modules can normally be grouped in either accounting or logistics. It is very rare that a consultant has in-depth knowledge of both sides. It is even more common that a consultant only masters one specific module. However, your marketability highly increases when you have a basic understanding of both accounting and logistics. Even better when you can demonstrate your skills by executing the *Register to Report (RTR)*, *Procure to Pay (PTP)* and *Order to Cash (OTC)* end-to-end business processes.

From a capability perspective, the consultants can have the ability to install, authorise, develop or configure SAP. It is very rare that a single consultant has multiple capabilities. It can happen that a consultant is able to develop and configure the system but in most cases, the consultant would not publicly advertise that they also can develop. Mainly because the rates to configure SAP ERP are much higher. And also being seen as a developer might lower their rate compared to someone only able to configure. Strange, but true. Those who can install or authorise often believe it takes too much effort to learn how to configure the system. A real shame, because it takes just some faith and commitment to make the quantum leap and expand your horizon.

It is highly likely that SAP experience is very fragmented within teams. You have developers with logistics know-how and configurers with only an accounting background. Building bridges between various sources of knowledge can be a real challenge. But the project would immediately benefit when everyone is able to configure the basic RTR, PTP and OTC processes in a standard SAP ERP system. Let me tell you why.

Imagine you are a senior SAP consultant who can configure OTC business scenarios. Some enhancements to the standard need to be developed. Assume you get a developer assigned who has no configuration experience. This person works to the best of his abilities, but he would struggle to test his own enhancements as it would be foreign to simulate end-to-end business processes. Instead he does a simple test and throws it over the wall in your direction. It is then up to you to validate his work.

Just as you can easily identify exceptional business cases, you can quickly find a range of issues. But you have no clue about the technical solution. So in return you give some notes and throw it back over the same wall towards the developer. This can turn into a long rally. Take into account that every throw over the wall could delay delivery by days. You can soon spend several weeks trying to make it work.

Imagine if the developer was able to configure OTC business processes. The quality of testing would immediately increase. Then this developer would be able to identify bugs and resolve them before you get involved. Even if that reduces the length of the rally by 50%, imagine how much faster you would be able to achieve results!

Peter Thompson has a very simple but effective "magic formula" to calculate your saving when you hire top quality consultants. You only need to answer two questions.

Q1: How many people do you employ that have access to the SAP ERP system?

A1: On average 20 people.

Q2: What would you guess is the average loss per person per month of efficiency, productivity and sales, due to lack of understanding of the SAP ERP system?

A2: On average £10,000 per person per month.

Based on the response to these two questions, your saving would be:

(20 * £10,000) * 12 = £2,400,000

When you know that education offers the opportunity to save £2,400,000 by increased efficiency and productivity, investment is a no brainer. This is why education is the last component of the **Fast Implementation Track™**. There is little point in cultivating Focus, Communication, Simplification or Commitment when you neglect Education.

PART THREE

9 ROAD TO SUCCESS

It is amazing how much people are willing to share during lunch. It is as if this precious time-out during the working day allows them to reflect. They only need someone they can trust in order to offload their frustrations.

The late morning meeting took much longer than planned, which is not really a surprise. But it was already past 1 o'clock and the restaurant staff were starting to clear up the food and beverages. There were plenty of seats to choose from. In the corner of my eye I noticed Kevin sitting by himself. Even though he almost finished his lunch, he waved at me.

Let me tell you about Kevin. He is the type of person you would not notice in a crowd, always wearing unbranded jeans, pastel coloured shirts and loafers. He is a hard worker and certainly one of the most experienced business analysts. Last month he celebrated his 23rd year of employment at the company. Not that many knew about that milestone.

But he likes it that way.

When I took the seat in front of him, I noticed that he hardly finished his plate and it seemed that the hot meal had already cooled down significantly. That gave me the impression he had something on his mind.

Over the past months we'd shared our thoughts about the project on many occasions, although normally we waited until we were at the hotel bar. It came as no surprise to me that there was another incident that preoccupied his mind. But this time he shared some news that I was not able to predict. A secret that he was about to reveal to the entire team later that day.

Kevin's main task was to oversee all teams in delivering the business requirements. That gave him the insight that each team was working in isolation. Any functionality that could be solved within the group was under control but as soon as the individual teams needed to work together to streamline an end-to-end business process, unforeseen complications emerged. Upon itself this was not a surprise. The more emphasis placed on delivering results, the more likely people focused on getting their ducks in a row. Even though this is normal human behaviour, it would not speed up the overall project delivery. Actually, quite the contrary.

Kevin was well aware that the common business goal was not on everyone's mind. No-one in particular was to blame other than upper management, because this goal was not well defined or communicated. And that bugged him. Like doing a puzzle without edges. His frustration actually gave birth to the first component of the **Fast Implementation Track™**. He was frustrated because he didn't have the means to communicate the biggest priority to his teams. Kevin understands now that you need to focus on the most important event within your business: the payment receipt of a customer invoice. Make sure all teams realise the importance of incoming cash flow. Then each team knows their task to ensure that this event can take place.

Unfortunately, at the time Kevin and I had no clear vision of the correct focus. Hence everyone defined their own focus, situated firmly within their comfort zone. Like the blind leading the blind. You can imagine that much valuable time was wasted as a result. A lack of leadership from upper management was certainly missing. This was also made clear by the fact that the management team and project resources were in located in different building, although on the same complex. The distance between decision makers and decision executioners was not just metaphorical.

Yes, there was a newsletter but hardly anyone read it. Yes, there were monthly team meetings but no-one was ever invited to contribute to any discussion. Kevin was not the type of person to share his thoughts to an entire auditorium. The project ran out of budget a while ago. That topic hijacked the monthly meeting several times as all kinds of managers made their speeches outlining their version of events, what it meant for the business and their new plans, which were in fact monologues. It became apparent that the only time their view was ever open for discussion was when they were actually phishing for the participants who would share only positive feedback. Kevin knew that any concerns should not be expressed at those times. It is much better to voice your opinions at the coffee machine afterwards.

There were no sessions that allowed mindstorming before brainstorming. That is a shame, because that is much more efficient than alienating your workforce. So many ideas never see the light of day. So much knowledge unused. What if there was a clear engagement strategy? Invite the team to discuss the decisions made and document the conclusions of that debate. Make sure decisions are translated into actions. Provide regular updates on the actions taken and their results, ensuring everyone has the ability to have a final say. It provides less distance between those funding the project and those responsible to make it happen. No hidden agendas and fewer traffic jams near the coffee machine. Kevin would have liked that structure, but he was not asked for his opinion on any improvements. Sure, there is a suggestion box. But he couldn't recall when an entry has ever been taken seriously enough to warrant any type of action. So why bother?

Kevin was well aware of the fact that SAP ERP implementation is not used to improve business processes. From the start, the steering committee made clear that we had to copy the current way of working. They probably didn't realise it would trigger a lot of enhancements to the standard system. Evidently there was enough money at the start of the project to allow this to happen. But now there was a black hole in the budget, which had been changing things over the past few months. The majority of the business requirements were in place so the question was raised, "Is it too late to revert back to standard?"

Even when a project is mid-flow, you might still be able to evaluate a change of tactic. When you have the correct focus, you can see to what extent your business is able to ensure their clients can be billed and that these invoices can be paid. It would be a bold move to make, but still worthwhile before you pass the point of no return. The safest option is to allow a few people to build a prototype with the aim to only use standard SAP functionality. This allows them to assess to what extent the company needs to change its processes and procedures to take advantage of SAP best practice. The closer to standard, the more simplified your solution, the more likely you can use this IT system to grow your business.

Many large scale IT projects run the risk of delivering as a type of Trojan Horse. At first glance, the solution may look suitable but then reveals itself as not fit for purpose after its introduction. Quite often this can be attributed to the countless additions to the standard system, many of them poorly documented. Then all the blood, sweat and tears and time and money is wasted. Some companies have the incentive to start all over, but not with a clean sheet. They often use the same people, likely to make the same mistakes and have no framework for planning and action, such as the **Fast Implementation Track™**. As if no hard lessons have been learnt.

If you want Kevin to entertain you for an entire evening, ask him about the involvement of the user community. He will tell you that the users haven't seen a single SAP screen yet. The project has been underway for two years! Obviously too early to share what's been done. Sense the irony. Not that it is his fault. He has been trying to convince the project management to perform site visits. But there was never sufficient budget for those travel arrangements. Actually, the management was scared to show anything at an early stage. They feared that end users might not like what they see. Instead, the project stayed in their ivory tower.

It would have made much more sense to involve the actual users as soon as possible. Of course you will find individuals who will complain, that is a given. But every complaint is an opportunity to exchange ideas. There seems to be far too much emphasis on getting it right the first time. People tend to forget that they are human. Being human means that you make mistakes. If you get it wrong, then you better identify this as soon as possible and learn from it. Apologise, make the necessary adjustments and move on.

This strategy will enhance the commitment from the user community. They feel that they can influence the end result. When their voice is heard and they see that action is taken, it is a win-win for everyone. Well, you certainly don't have to convince Kevin of that. He secretly organises video conferences with a select group of users. All these discussions have been energising and constructive. But he would prefer to do these in clear daylight.

A moment of silence. Kevin was deliberating whether or not to tell me what was on his mind. We were now the only two people in the restaurant. Our plates had been collected by the staff and they were closing down and preparing for the tomorrow's breakfast. Amongst everything that had happened over the past years, Kevin only had one regret. He should have never joined this project. His confession surprised me.

Even before the project started, his manager asked him to be part of a SAP ERP project. Kevin was surprised by the offer, as he did not have any SAP knowledge. However, that was not a problem. He knew how the current system worked as he was one of the people who designed it. So his insight was of monumental value. Plus, he was assured that he would learn SAP, the worldwide leading software solution for ERP. That promise made Kevin decide to join. Sadly, he has never been able to learn SAP because budget for team education was never allocated. It appeared to be an empty promise. One of many, but this time it was the proverbial drip that overflowed the bucket. As the project seemed to be out of budget and he was not getting any younger, he had decided to leave the company.

My jaw dropped.

That morning, Kevin had informed the project manager that he'd accepted a new position at a company closer to his home. Same type of work, different industry. He'd already received confirmation of his first training session at SAP.

The initial response from his project manager was typical, as Kevin's departure was identified as a project risk. There was no interest to explore what drove Kevin to leave prematurely. Not the type of feedback Kevin expected. But it was a confirmation that he made the right decision.

The real sense of loss came later that afternoon, when the rumours of Kevin's departure spread while we were still at the restaurant. A colleague actually tracked us down for confirmation. That moment was memorable. Honest sadness from both sides, with an understanding that it was a sensible decision. Kevin would be truly missed by his team, a lot of whom were also dissatisfied with their roles at the company. It is such a shame that valuable employees feel the need to move on. Kevin certainly did not want to move jobs, but as his company made a saving in education, the loss of experience is going to cost them dearly.

Hopefully you now see the benefits when embracing the **Fast Implementation Track™**. Let me discuss the 5 components one final time.

The secret to successful SAP ERP implementation can be summarised with a simple sentence containing seven words. The **Fast Implementation Track™** is a way to engage the entire business in achieving that overall objective. It is easy to remember and easy to apply. It has been tested and proved and verified by several dozens of self-made millionaires. It is based on common sense that is not common knowledge. You can guess this sentence when asking yourself what event is vital within your business focus on avoiding bankruptcy.

Always have enough money in the bank.
~Isard Haasakker

This sentence cannot be misinterpreted by anyone in your team. Make sure you communicate without ambiguity. You can make a very convincing speech, but it can still result in debate and confusion. When you hear, "The burglar threatened the student with the knife", who is holding the knife? When you read, "Someone saw an elephant in their pyjamas this morning", was the elephant wearing clothes? How about the stolen picture that was found by a tree? How can red tape hold up a bridge? What happened when a newspaper reported, "Police help dog bite victim"? The professor said he was glad to be a man, and so is his wife. The chicken wasn't ready to eat, because it was served in a hot bowl of soup.

A common mistake is to let complexity take over. Essential decisions are either not made or postponed. This allows temporary solutions to remain in place until the end of time. It takes authority, conviction and courage to discover, discuss and apply simplicity amongst complexity. Quite often this coincides with endless management meetings, triggering numerous requests for analysis to sustain the status quo. In the meantime, the deadline for deployment comes closer and slowly, panic, apathy and desolation creeps into the team. This is the moment when professionals also feel that their advice is not taken seriously, wondering whether the grass is greener at the other side.

The main reason for identified complexity can also be linked to the challenge to successfully apply change management. Up until now, each department in your organisation has had the opportunity to optimise their own processes. Now all departments are forced to cooperate on a level never experienced before. For many, this is translated as a loss of precious functionality. It is therefore to be expected that there will be resistance to change.

Your task is to guide your business through this transition. Show that this change is real and not just an empty promise. Make your entire organisation believe in the change they will undergo. Communicating sacrifices is necessary in order to simplify to multiply. Being able to multiply your business is the best strategy to keep everyone employed. For sure, this clear message transforms opposition into commitment.

There is still one important hurdle to overcome. This relates in the investment to educate your workforce. It is shocking to see how often it gets neglected. Any person experiences a boost of confidence by learning and applying new skills. However, many managers worry that the time spent on education during regular working hours will be potentially detrimental in achieving project milestones on time. Instead, they do not realise that lack of knowledge is the main reason why these deadlines are not met.

You need a team that has a wide knowledge of all the vital business processes. This is applicable not only to those configuring the system, but also to the developers and the team arranging the user authorisations. There is even a case to be made for involving the technical infrastructure experts as well. The main objective is to ensure that everyone is able to test their own work in isolation. Widening your comfort zone prevents silo-thinking and automatically increases collaboration to achieve a common goal. This may sound trivial, but it is the basis for increased efficiency and productivity.

The size of the budget to implement SAP ERP does not matter. A successful project achieves its goals on time and within budget. In the past, I have been part of victorious projects with a budget between £200,000 and £60,000,000. What did they have in common? In both projects, the **Fast Implementation Track™** was adhered to successfully.

FOCUS on the business processes linked to the customer invoice payment receipt. The most important event in your business.

COMMUNICATE this focus and ensure that everyone understands its importance. This is how you avoid syntax ambiguity.

SIMPLIFY your business processes, only deviating from standard when there is a good reason. Remember, you need to simplify before you can multiply your business growth.

COMMIT your business to embrace SAP ERP as the new tool to run your business. Change becomes reality once others commit to your vision.

EDUCATE your workforce before, during and after implementing SAP ERP. The best strategy to increase efficiency, productivity, commitment and collaboration.

ABOUT THE AUTHOR

Isard Haasakker, founder and director of No Tie Generation believes that *there is no tool for development more effective than self-empowerment.*
The brands Isard has created, his company image and his mission place this ethos at their heart.

In authoring "Make F.I.T. Your Purpose" and creating the **Fast Implementation Track™**, Isard provides an innovative and accessible platform where both employers and employees can harness valuable resources which will empower them to do what they always dreamed of.

His passion is to help his clients to achieve what they never thought possible. This is trailblazing his thought-leadership path in the industry and makes him the go-to expert for SAP ERP implementation and support.

After 20 years being a SAP consultant, Isard now focuses on transforming his skills to coach entrepreneurs and business leaders to successfully implement and support their SAP ERP systems. His understanding of the entrepreneurial mindset uniquely qualifies him to bridge gaps in communication across different departments. He will focus on the areas most important to your business' success, and deliver an end result which provides you with self-sufficiency, a bird's-eye perspective and significantly increased free time and money.

This book is just the beginning.

Visit **makeFITyourPurpose.com** to stay up-to-date
with the latest **Fast Implementation Track™**
developments, including additional products and
services to meet your business needs

www.ingramcontent.com/pod-product-compliance
Lightning Source LLC
Chambersburg PA
CBHW051207050326
40689CB00008B/1230